D1454408

THE SECRET WORLD OF

Whales

THE SECRET WORLD OF
Whales

Theresa Greenaway

Raintree

www.raintreepublishers.co.uk
Visit our website to find out more information about **Raintree** books.

To order:
 Phone 44 (0) 1865 888112
 Send a fax to 44 (0) 1865 314091
 Visit the Raintree Bookshop at www.raintreepublishers.co.uk to browse our catalogue and order online.

First published in Great Britain by Raintree,
Halley Court, Jordan Hill, Oxford
OX2 8EJ, part of Harcourt Education.
Raintree is a registered trademark of Harcourt Education Ltd.

Produced for Raintree by Discovery Books
Editors: Helen Dwyer and Catherine Clarke
Series Consultant: Michael Chinery
Design: Ian Winton
Illustrations: Stuart Lafford
Production: Jonathan Smith

Originated by Dot Gradations Ltd
Printed and bound in China by South China Printing Company

ISBN 1 844 21591 1
07 06 05 04 03
10 9 8 7 6 5 4 3 2 1

British Library Cataloguing in Publication Data
Greenaway, Theresa
The Secret World of Whales
599.5
A full catalogue record for this book is available from the British Library.

Acknowledgements
The publishers would like to thank the following for permission to reproduce photographs:
Bruce Coleman Collection pp.9, **10** (Pacific Stock), **11** (Mark Carwardine), **12/13** (Pacific Stock), **15** (Gunter Ziesler), **16** (Mark Carwardine), **19** (Bill Wood), **21/25** (Mark Carwardine), **30/32** (Pacific Stock), **33** (E. Bjurstrom), **34**, **38** (Pacific Stock), **40** (Mark Carwardine), **41** (Pacific Stock), **43** (Jeff Foott); Natural History Photographic Agency pp.**18** (Haroldo Palo Jr), **19** (Norbert Wu), **28** (A.N.T), **36** (Daniel Heuclin), **37** (David E. Myers), **39** (Trevor McDonald); Oxford Scientific Films pp.**8** (Gerard Soury), **14** (Howard Hall), **17** (Daniel J.Cox), **22** (Kim Westerkov), **23** (Doug Allan), **26** (Norbert Wu), **29** (Howard Hall), **31** (Doug Allan), **35** (Tui de Roy), **42** (Tony Martins).
All background images © Steck-Vaughn Collection (Corbis Royalty Free, Getty Royalty Free, and StockBYTE).

Cover photograph reproduced with permission of the Bruce Coleman Collection.

Any words appearing in the text in bold, **like this**, are explained in the Glossary.

Contents

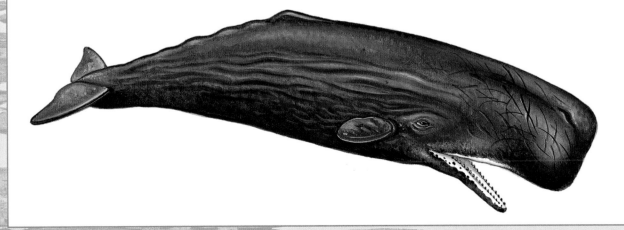

Back to the sea

Just like humans, whales are **warm-blooded**, air-breathing **mammals** that feed their young with milk from their own body. Millions of years ago, the **ancestors** of whales had four limbs (arms or legs). They walked on land, searching for food near rivers and seas. As they spent more and more time in the water, their bodies changed, until they were able to live in water all the time. Whales now live, feed, **mate** and give birth in water, although they still have to come to the surface to breathe.

dorsal fin
The **dorsal fin** of a humpback is small compared to its large body. Some whales have no dorsal fin at all.

- The blue whale is the largest animal that has ever lived. The longest male ever found was 31 metres long, and the longest female, 33 metres.

- The blue whale is also very heavy. An average-sized blue whale weighs 80–120 tonnes, but a really big one can weigh as much as 150 tonnes.

- Right whales and bowhead whales weigh on average from 30 to 80 tonnes

- The sperm whale is the largest toothed whale.

- The smallest whale is the Gulf of California harbour porpoise, which is also known as the Vaquita or Cochito. Its maximum length is 1.4 metres.

- The bowhead whale has the longest plates of baleen.

tail fluke
A broad horizontal fin used to push the whale through the water.

There are about 80 different kinds, or **species**, of whales. They are all **carnivores**, eating a variety of other sea animals. Whales are divided into two groups: those with teeth, and those that have horny plates, called baleen, instead of teeth. There are ten kinds of **baleen whales** – the group that includes most of the really large whales, such as the blue, bowhead and humpback whales. All the other kinds of whales, including dolphins and porpoises, are **toothed whales**. Many dolphins and porpoises are small, although some kinds, such as the killer whale (orca) and pilot whale, are quite large.

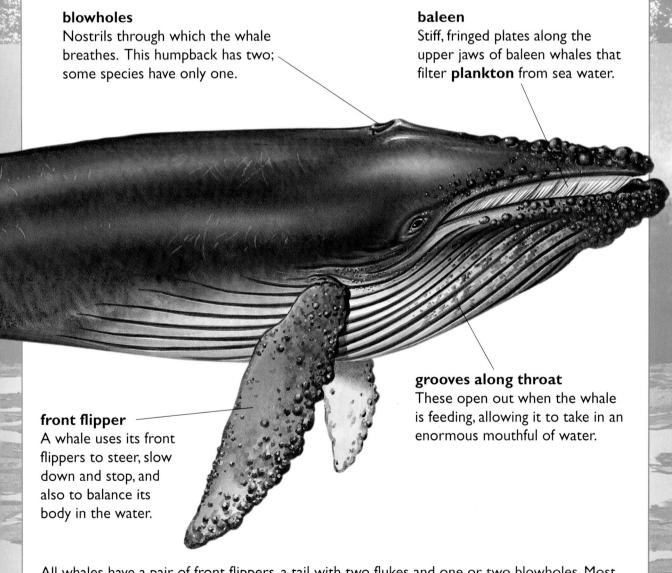

blowholes
Nostrils through which the whale breathes. This humpback has two; some species have only one.

baleen
Stiff, fringed plates along the upper jaws of baleen whales that filter **plankton** from sea water.

grooves along throat
These open out when the whale is feeding, allowing it to take in an enormous mouthful of water.

front flipper
A whale uses its front flippers to steer, slow down and stop, and also to balance its body in the water.

All whales have a pair of front flippers, a tail with two flukes and one or two blowholes. Most, but not all, have a dorsal fin. Only baleen whales have plates of baleen along their upper jaws, and only the **rorquals** have long grooves along the throat, as seen in this humpback whale.

The right whale filters **plankton** from sea water through its baleen. The lump on its head is rough skin, to which barnacles (small sea animals with shells) often cling.

Whales have a **streamlined** shape. Instead of arms they have wide flippers, and they have no legs. Most **species** have a **dorsal fin** on their backs. Others, such as the sperm whale and the humpback, have a ridge of lumps along their backs, but the right and bowhead whales have neither. The tail is made up of a pair of wide, horizontal fins called **flukes**.

A whale's head is different from a land **mammal's** head. Whales do not have large outer ears. Instead, a whale's ears are just a tiny hole on each side of its head. A whale has small eyes, and most can see underwater and in air. A whale breathes in air through one or two nostrils that are on the top of its head. These are called **blowholes**.

BALEEN WHALES

Baleen whales do not have any teeth. Instead, they have plates made of a tough substance called keratin. These plates hang side by side along the upper jaws. They are called baleen. Each plate has a fringe of fibres (threads) down one side. Like our fingernails and hair, which are also made of keratin, baleen plates grow all the time, so as they wear away, new ones take their place. The baleen is used during feeding to strain small sea animals from sea water.

TOOTHED WHALES

All **toothed whales** have teeth, but the number of teeth varies by species. Dolphins have many teeth on both the upper and lower jaws. The long-snouted spinner dolphin has the most of all – sometimes as many as 260! Some types of **beaked whales**, such as the narwhal, have just two teeth. Only one of the narwhal's teeth is usually seen. This grows into a very long tusk, but the other tooth stays small and hidden in the whale's mouth.

Like those of this killer whale, most whales' teeth are cone-shaped. These sharply pointed teeth are good at gripping wriggling or slippery **prey** but cannot chew or grind food.

The colouring of this spotted dolphin makes it harder for **predators** to see it against the light and shadow created by sunlight on the water.

are marked with spots. The common dolphin is the most colourful whale, with patches of yellow as well as black, white and grey.

Individual whales are easy to **identify**, even out at sea. The right whale has patches of thickened skin on its head, which are slightly different from whale to whale. Each humpback whale has its own pattern of white markings on the underside of its tail **flukes**. These can be seen when the whale lifts its tail above the surface of the sea.

COLOUR AND PATTERN

Whales have smooth, almost hairless skin. Most whales are grey in colour, but the beluga is white and the bowhead whale is completely black except for a white chin. Many dolphins, including the killer whale, are patterned in black, grey and white. Some, such as the roughtooth and spotted dolphin,

▲ The patches of rough skin on the right whale vary in shape and position. This means that each of these whales can be recognized.

◀ As the humpback whale dives, its huge tail lifts clear of the water, so the pattern on the underside of each fluke can be seen.

WHERE THEY LIVE

Whales live in seas and oceans all around the world. They live in the cold waters of the Arctic and Antarctic, as well as in warm, **tropical** oceans. The larger whales are animals of the deep oceans, although some follow the line of the coast, especially when travelling long distances. Smaller whales, such as most dolphins, pilot whales and **beaked whales**, also swim far out to sea, but humpback dolphins and porpoises

As the common dolphin leaps clear of the water, the 'hourglass' pattern on its side comes into view. The yellow colour may fade in winter.

are among those that stay in shallow coastal waters, harbours, and river **estuaries**. There are even five dolphin **species** that live in freshwater rivers.

How can a blue whale be so big?

It would not be possible for a land animal to be as large as a blue whale. Its bones would break under its huge weight. Because water supports the weight of a swimming animal, even a large whale is almost weightless in sea water, so its bones are not overloaded. A whale's bones are actually quite light. Inside each bone is a network of large spaces that are filled with oils and fatty substances that help it float.

I DIDN'T KNOW THAT

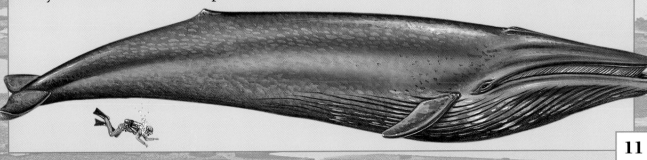

Swimming and diving

Whales move by swimming. They are unable to move over land, although some kinds of dolphins can ride waves right to the edge of the shore to catch **prey** and then wriggle back into deeper water. Whales, including dolphins and porpoises, swim by propelling (pushing) themselves through the water with their muscular tail and two broad fins, or **flukes**.

The upwards stroke of the tail, called the power stroke, pushes the whale forward. Then the tail moves downwards, so that it is in the right position to make another power stroke. When a whale wants to swim slowly, it makes slow, deep

The humpback whale lifts its massive tail to push itself forwards through the water.

Large baleen whales cruise at speeds from 5 to 20 kilometres (3–12 miles) per hour, and some, such as the blue whale, can reach speeds of 48 kilometres (30 miles) per hour over short distances.

A sei whale can reach a speed of 56 kilometres (35 miles) per hour over short distances.

Dolphins swimming fast reach speeds of 48–56 kilometres (30–35 miles) per hour.

Grey whale migration is a tourist attraction in California, USA, where whales can be seen swimming slowly just a short distance offshore.

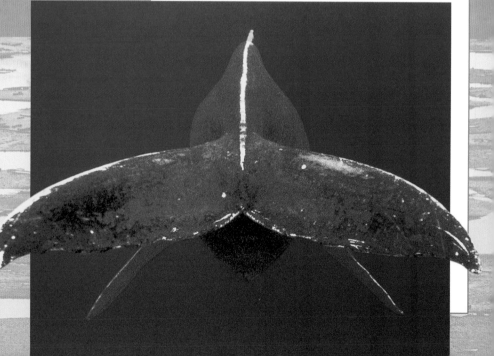

strokes with its tail. If it wants to go faster, it makes faster but shallower strokes, beating its tail about twice a second. Its smooth skin and **streamlined** shape help it to move easily as it swims through the water.

As the whale glides forwards, it uses its flippers to prevent it from rolling from side to side in the water. Flippers also help a whale to change direction, slow down and stop.

BOW-RIDING
Swimming requires energy, and swimming fast means that even more energy has to be used. Dolphins save energy by using the waves made by the bows (fronts) of boats and ships as they cut through the water. By getting their bodies and tail flukes in the right position, dolphins use the energy in the bow wave to move themselves forward

Whales often throw themselves completely clear of the water, landing with a huge splash. This is called **breaching**. No one knows exactly why whales do this. It could be that they are simply playing!

faster. **Species** such as bottlenose, striped and common dolphins often bow-ride in this way.

13

KEEPING WARM

Like all **mammals**, whales are **warm-blooded**. This means their body temperature remains fairly constant. They must be able to keep warm, especially when they are swimming in the cold seas near **polar** regions.

To avoid losing heat, whales have a thick layer of fat, just below the skin, known as **blubber**. This blubber stops them losing heat from their blood and muscles. A bowhead whale has a layer of blubber that can be as much as 50 centimetres thick.

If it swims fast for a while, a whale may become too hot. When this happens, it reduces its temperature by increasing the blood flow to its flippers, **flukes** and head. In these parts of its body, there is almost no blubber, and so the sea water cools the whale's blood.

I DIDN'T KNOW THAT

Deep dives

To dive, whales take a series of huge breaths and plunge beneath the surface. Most do not go down far, but sperm whales make incredible dives almost to 1000 metres. Large males may stay underwater for up to 2 hours, although most sperm whale dives last about 10 minutes. Sperm whales make almost vertical dives. Recent films have shown that they rest very still in a vertical position with their heads pointing downwards.

ANNUAL MIGRATION

The large **baleen whales** make long journeys each year. They spend the summer in **polar** waters, feeding on **schools** of krill, an animal related to shrimps and small fish. In winter, they travel to warmer waters nearer the **equator** to **mate** or give birth. Of the **toothed whales**, only male sperm

Unlike most other whales, some belugas, such as those that live in the Gulf of St Lawrence on Canada's eastern coast, do not migrate as the seasons change.

whales make a similar **migration**. They spend summer feeding on squid in colder waters nearer the polar ice, but swim to warmer seas in winter. Females spend all year in warmer water.

Breathing

Whales have to come to the surface to breathe in air. If they cannot do this, they will drown. A whale's nostrils are on the top of its head. This is different from other **mammals** that live in water, such as seals, which have nostrils at the tips of their snouts. A whale's nostrils form a single or double **blowhole**. Whales close the blowhole while underwater, so that water cannot get in.

When a whale needs to take a breath, it pushes the blowhole above the water and opens it. Air is breathed out at great pressure,

This humpback whale, like other **baleen whales**, has a double blowhole. These are only open when the whale breaks the surface to breathe.

A whale breathes two to four times a minute while moving at the surface. (People breathe about fifteen times a minute.)

The air the whale breathes out has almost all the oxygen (98 per cent) removed from it.

Male sperm whales can stay underwater for over 2 hours, but females stay underwater for only about 40 minutes.

Dolphins dive to depths of about 280 metres and can stay underwater for about 8 minutes.

When a baleen whale surfaces to breathe, it makes 10–15 spouts, 15 seconds apart.

sending a fountain of water vapour (gas), **mucus** and oily droplets into the air. This is called a spout or blow. The spout of a large whale is easy to see from far away because it rises high into the air. The water vapour becomes water droplets as it meets cool air.

Whales are able to open their mouths during dives with no fear of drowning because there is no way that water from their mouths can

The spout of a humpback whale. A wide fountain of air and water vapour spouts about 3 metres into the air.

enter their lungs. Most mammals can breathe either through the nose or through the mouth, but a whale can only breathe through its nostrils. Its air passages are not connected to the tubes that take food from the mouth to the stomach. Because of this, whales can catch and swallow food while they are underwater.

17

Baleen whales have two nostrils. When they breathe out, a jet of air and water vapour comes from each. In some **species** these stay separate, but in others they join into a single spout. The spout of many of these whales is so recognizable that it can be used to **identify** exactly which kind of whale it is. The blue whale makes a tall, thin fountain of spray. The right whale makes two wide spouts of vapour (gas).

The spout from each blowhole of the right whale goes in a different direction, making a unique V-shaped blow.

Toothed whales have single **blowholes**. Except for sperm whales and killer whales, toothed whales hardly ever make a spout large enough to be seen from a distance. The sperm whale is **unique** among whales because its blowhole is at the tip of its huge head and slightly to the left.

LUNGS

A whale's lungs are very efficient. A whale nearly empties its lungs when it breathes out, and almost completely fills them every time it breathes in. This means that almost all of the old air in its

Oxygen reserves

When a whale dives, it stores nearly all the **oxygen** its body needs in its muscles and blood. Oxygen is shifted to the most important organs – the lungs, heart and brain. This explains why a surfacing whale does not suffer from the often fatal condition known as 'the bends', which is a kind of **nitrogen** poisoning that affects human divers when they come up too quickly. The whale is holding its breath while it dives and resurfaces, which means that the pressure of the water does not force nitrogen into its bloodstream as it breathes. Human divers suffer the bends because they breathe air – which includes nitrogen – while underwater.

lungs is exchanged for fresh air with every breath. In comparison, a human exchanges only about 10–20 per cent of the amount of air in his or her lungs with every breath. Whales can breathe in and out much faster than people do – a fin whale breathes out all old air and breathes in fresh air in less than 2 seconds. **Rorquals**, which do not dive very deeply, take 3 or 4 breaths and are then able to dive for up to 10 minutes.

Senses and navigation

A whale's senses allow it to understand what is happening in its watery world. This is vital to its survival, as it uses its senses to find food, escape from danger and recognize a possible **mate**. Whales can see and hear, but under the water their sense of hearing is more important to them than their eyesight. Sound travels 4.5 times faster in water than it does in air. Light does not travel nearly as well in water as it does in air.

The eyes of this grey whale are about 2 metres from the top of its snout. In spite of the small size of their eyes, most whales have good eyesight above water.

Very little daylight reaches the depths to which sperm whales dive. The only light in this darkness comes from sea creatures that can produce their own.

Although the noise made by a blue whale is the loudest sound produced by any animal alive today – louder even than a jet aeroplane – it is a very low noise – too low to be heard by human ears.

Dolphins can make more than 3000 clicking sounds per second.

With their clicks, dolphins are able to locate tiny fish only 2 centimetres long.

Whales do not have a sense of smell, but some toothed whales can taste their food and the water in which they are swimming using taste buds on their tongues.

Only 10 per cent of the light at the surface reaches down as far as 10 metres in clear water.

Whales use sound in a number of ways in their daily lives. All whales produce a variety of whistles, moans, chirps or thumps that they use to communicate with each other. With all these many noises they can let each other know where they are, whether they have

These spotted dolphins communicate with each other and work together as a group to round up **schools** of small fish that they feed on near the surface.

found food, if they are hurt or **stranded** or if they are looking for a mate. In addition, **toothed whales** make noises when they are gathering for a hunt. Toothed whales also produce streams of clicks that they use to find their way around and locate **prey**.

SPY-HOPPING

Whales can see both above and below water. Many will stand upright in the water with their heads above the surface. In this position they can look around to see if there are fishing boats or other ships near by. This habit is known as **spy-hopping**. The grey whale, the beluga, pilot whales, the killer whale and Risso's dolphin are among the **species** known to spy-hop.

HEARING

Mammals have a pair of inner ears inside their heads that receive sound waves. Sound reaches the inner ear of land animals through openings in the head which are usually surrounded by a large, often furry, outer ear. A whale's ears are different. There is no outer ear, and the opening on the side of the head is tiny and plugged with wax. The inner ears are in holes filled with a foamy substance.

Exactly how sound travels from the water through a whale's head to its inner ears is not yet known. Scientists think that low sounds may travel along the tube leading from each ear opening. They think that higher sounds travel along oily channels in the lower jaw and other bones of **toothed whales** to reach the inner ears.

When whales such as these killer whales want to know what is going on, they can stand upright with the front part of their bodies right out of the water. They need to turn their whole body around to look in all directions.

MAKING A NOISE

Whales communicate with each other by making an amazing variety of noises. Some of these are outside the range of human hearing, but others can be heard clearly. In the past, whalers (whale-hunters) could **identify** some whales from the sounds they made.

The very low sounds made by **baleen whales** travel enormous distances through the water. Using these sounds as messages is the way in which individual baleen whales keep in contact with others of their own kind.

Sailors called the beluga 'the sea canary' because its tuneful underwater 'chatter' could be heard clearly aboard ship.

SONG OF THE WHALE

In 1970, a US record company produced a very unusual recording. It was a sequence of sounds made by a single, male humpback whale. The 'songs' of the male humpback are made up of many different patterns of sounds, so that each song may last 6–30 minutes. Male humpbacks have been known to sing one song after another for up to 24 hours. These songs can be heard by other humpbacks over 30 kilometres (19 miles) away.

Using echolocation, a toothed whale can scan all around it, even in complete darkness, to find and avoid obstacles, to find **schools** of fish, and even to home in on one fish or squid.

ECHOLOCATION

Toothed whales have an inbuilt system that helps them to know what is around them and to find food. This system is called **echolocation**. When sound waves hit an object, an echo bounces back. We can hear echoes of our voices if we shout in a cave or a steep-sided valley. Dolphins and other toothed whales can make a steady stream of clicking sounds that pass out through a fatty lump called a melon, near the back of the upper jaw. The melon focuses the stream of clicks into a beam.

The sound waves hit underwater objects such as rocks, fishing nets and fish, producing another stream of rebounding echoes. This is picked up by, and passes through, the toothed whale's lower jaw and into its inner ear. The hearing of these whales is extremely sensitive to these echoes. They can tell the difference between objects, and know where they are, from the kind of echoes that they hear.

I DIDN'T KNOW THAT

River dolphins

There are five **species** of river dolphins. They live in the major rivers of South America (the Amazon and the Orinoco); India, Pakistan and Bangladesh (the Indus and the Ganges); and China (the Yangtze). All five species are very rare, and all five have very poor eyesight.

Food and feeding

All whales, from the largest **baleen whales** to the smallest porpoises, are **predators** that need to catch live **prey**. How they do this, and what kinds of prey they catch, varies from **species** to species. The largest baleen whales eat some of the smallest animals! Baleen whales are filter feeders. They filter, or strain, small fish and other tiny animals swimming near the surface of the sea by passing large quantities of water through their bristly plates of baleen.

Toothed whales are more active hunters, often working in groups to round up a **school** of fish and then taking turns to catch their fill.

This bottlenose dolphin will soon catch and eat any fish that are not quite as fit as the rest.

 A blue whale's huge mouth holds up to about 70,000 litres of water.

 Sei whales, which can measure up to 15 metres long, use their baleen plates to filter out tiny living creatures less than 1.25 centimetres long.

 A blue whale eats around 40 million krill (a shrimp-like animal) every day. That's 4 tonnes of krill.

 An adult sperm whale eats 1 tonne of food a day.

 The killer whale regularly catches the largest prey of all whales – sea lions, manta rays and seals.

They may have to chase their prey fast in order to catch it. The teeth of most toothed whales are sharp and pointed to catch and hold on to slippery fish and squid, but these teeth cannot cut up or grind food, so almost all of these whales swallow their prey whole. Porpoises are an exception. They have knife-shaped teeth that are able to cut chunks off the larger fish that they catch on the bed of shallow coastal waters.

FILTER FEEDERS

When a baleen whale feeds, it takes in a mouthful of water, together with all the **plankton** that it contains. As it closes its mouth, the whale's huge tongue pushes up, forcing the water out of the sides of the mouth through the baleen plates. The fringed edges of the baleen plates form a mat of fibres (threads) on each side of the mouth. When the mouth is completely shut, the whale swallows its catch.

HOW A BALEEN WHALE FEEDS

1. The whale takes in a mouthful of water. **Rorqual** whales, such as the whale shown in this illustration, have deep grooves along their throats that expand to allow the whale to take in a huge amount of water at one time.

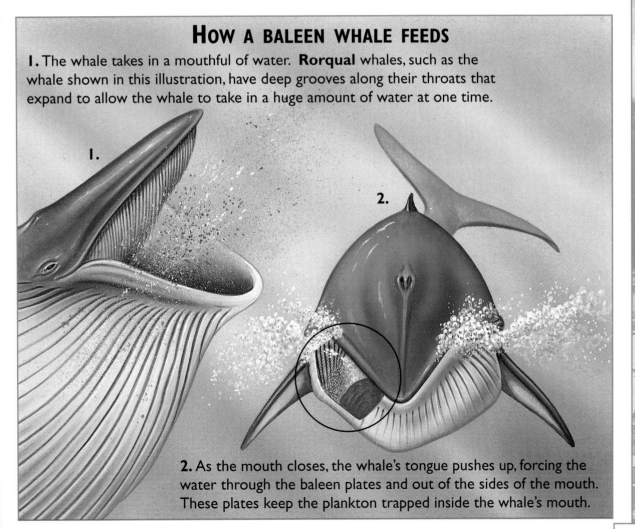

2. As the mouth closes, the whale's tongue pushes up, forcing the water through the baleen plates and out of the sides of the mouth. These plates keep the plankton trapped inside the whale's mouth.

Rorquals are baleen whales that have grooves along their throats – like the humpback in this picture. These grooves allow the whale's throat to expand enormously when it feeds.

Baleen whales do not all filter out food in exactly the same way. The grey whale stirs up the mud and sand on the seabed with its snout. Then it takes a mouthful of the sandy or muddy water and filters out all the small animals it has uncovered through rows of short, stiff plates of baleen. Right and bowhead whales have deep lower lips that curve up, hiding very long baleen plates. These whales swim along slowly with their mouths open, straining **plankton** from the water as it passes through the two 'curtains' of baleen.

EXPERT HUNTERS

The killer whale, also known as the orca, is the only whale that eats **warm-blooded prey** such as seals, dolphins and penguins. Killer whales also eat squid, bony fish and sharks. A group of five to ten orcas in **polar** regions may **spy-hop** to see if there is a seal sitting on a small **ice floe**. When they find one, they all swim towards the floe together, turning sideways as they get nearer. This sends a large wave over the ice, washing the seal into the water, and into the waiting jaws of another killer whale. Although killer whale teeth cannot slice chunks off their prey, they can tear it apart by tossing it into the air again and again.

On the menu

The sperm whale feeds mostly on squid that it catches at depths ranging from 1 metre down to more than 900 metres. These large whales also eat a variety of other slow-moving prey, including bottom-feeding sharks, skates, jellyfish and angler fish. Other more unexpected items have also been found inside their stomachs, including coconuts, boots and even a bucket!

I DIDN'T KNOW THAT

Reproduction

There is still a lot that we do not know about how some kinds of whales choose their **mates**. Even the biggest of them all, the blue whale, has kept its courting behaviour a secret from us. We also know little about the courtship of **beaked whales**.

Others are not so shy. Males and females of the great right whale start their energetic courtship by leaping out of the water and

Courting humpback whales are very energetic. They chase each other through the water and make loud splashes with their tails.

Gestation, which is the length of time it takes for a whale to develop inside its mother before birth, lasts from 8 to 16 months, depending on the species.

A newborn blue whale can be up to 7.8 metres long and usually weighs about 3 tonnes.

A mother blue whale usually produces about 200 litres of milk a day for her offspring.

A blue whale calf gains about 90 kilograms a day for the first week of its life.

breaching again and again. Humpbacks chase each other, splashing with their tails. Longfin pilot whales head-butt each other. Bottlenose dolphins swim close together, touching each other with their flippers. Some of the singing of male humpback whales may be a way of attracting females.

Male whales compete with each other in order to win mates. When it is time for sperm whales to mate, the males travel to the females, which live together in small groups in warm seas near the **equator**. The largest males battle fiercely. They charge each other

Male narwhals fight with their long, sharp tusks. Injuries are common, and tusks often get broken.

head-on, then grip each other's lower jaws and wrestle. Often, they break teeth or even the lower jaw itself in the process.

Male narwhals fight with their long, spirally-twisted tusks, which can grow to 3 metres in length. Such trials of strength may be little more than show, but male narwhals sometimes carry the scars from these battles for the rest of their lives. Beaked whale males also fight fiercely, lashing out at each other with their teeth.

BIRTH

Whales and dolphins **mate** either at the surface or just below the water. After mating, the young whale develops inside its mother's body for many months until it is ready to be born. Blue whale **calves** are often born tail first, while killer whales are often born head first. As soon as it is born, the female helps her calf to the surface so it can breathe. Like other

A humpback calf feeds from its mother for its first year of life. During this time, the calf stays close to its mother for protection.

mammals, female whales feed their young from their own body, providing a rich, fatty milk.

A NEW LIFE

When it has taken its first breath, and had its first meal, a newborn whale is able to follow its mother.

The calf has to feed underwater between breaths. The milk is pumped from the mother's body to help the young calf to feed and grow quickly.

GROWING UP

By the time it is half grown, the calf no longer needs to feed from its mother, but it may stay with her for longer. Young calves are very playful, nipping their mother's tail **flukes** and wriggling over her back. Mothers guard their calves if a **predator** threatens. A grey whale mother may even lift a young calf out of danger with a flipper.

Life is fun for a young dolphin, but it is hard work as well. The calf has to learn how to catch its own fish and to recognize and avoid danger.

Although small whales, such as porpoises or dolphins, can **mate** at a young age (3–5 years old for females, 6–8 years old for males), this does not mean they are fully grown. It takes many years for a large whale to reach its full size. A male great sperm whale is not fully grown until it is 35 years old. Porpoises may live for up to 23 years, some dolphins up to 50 years and some of the larger whales live even longer than that. A sperm whale can live for 70 years, while a humpback generally lives to 40 or so. It is believed that some fin whales can live to be 100 years old.

A FAMILY GROUP

Northern bottlenose whales are among those that live all year in a family group of about six whales. Each group contains one adult male and a small number of females and their **calves**. Killer whales live in family groups of five to twenty. One-fifth of these are adult males, but there is only one dominant (leading) male. He is easy to spot because he has the longest **dorsal fin**.

In this group of killer whales, five males with tall, upright dorsal fins can be seen. The shorter, more curved fin of a female killer whale is on the far left.

Slow reproduction

Whales reproduce slowly. Porpoises have one calf every two years. Female whales of many **species** may produce only one calf every three or four years. This means that a female bottlenose dolphin with a life of about 35 years will give birth to just 8 calves.

Social skills

Most whales are social animals that seem to enjoy being with other whales, whether they live close to each other all year or travel great distances. Scientists have learned that the way whales communicate with each other is very complicated. Studying animals in the wild is the best way of learning about them, but in the case of whales, which spend all their time roaming the oceans, this can be very difficult.

A group of whales is known as a pod.

Unlike most baleen whales, fin whales live in groups, which number from 3 to 20 animals.

A school of common dolphins may contain hundreds of members.

Many kinds of dolphins, including killer whales, can be kept in **captivity** in aquariums and sea life centres. Although many people think that it is unkind to keep dolphins in captivity it has allowed scientists to study them more easily than in the wild. Much has been learned about dolphin intelligence and **echolocation** as a result of this kind of study. Dolphins and killer whales in captivity amaze all who go to see them. They are quick to learn tricks, and to copy the activities of other **mammals**, including humans.

This killer whale is performing a routine it has learned in a sea life centre in California, USA.

WORKING TOGETHER

Dolphins and other whales that live in groups help each other to perform many tasks. They work together during a hunt, rounding up **schools** of fish. Females often help each other during birth. Some have been seen gently tugging on the tail **flukes** of a baby to speed up a birth. Once the **calf** is born, a number of females help the mother to nudge the calf to the surface so it can breathe. Dolphins often work together to warn each other of approaching **predators**.

A group of humpbacks blows a 'net' of bubbles to drive a school of fish close together. Then they lunge up to the surface with their mouths open, each whale scooping up many fish.

CARE OF THE SICK

A whale that cannot reach the surface of the water will drown. Dolphins and other whales quickly sense signs of distress in their own and other **species**. They push the injured animal to the surface so it can breathe. There are even stories of dolphins coming to the aid of a drowning person. The larger whales also answer distress signals from others of their own kind. If one is injured, others surround it to protect it from attack by other **predators**.

I DIDN'T KNOW THAT

Friendly dolphins

The friendly nature of bottlenose dolphins delights many people who go to see them in aquariums. People are able to feed some of them fish from their hands, as well as watch them performing tricks such as leaping through hoops above the water. Occasionally, wild dolphins look for people swimming in the sea and seem to enjoy their company. Along parts of the south-west coast of the UK in the mid-1970s, a male bottlenose dolphin became famous for coming close to shore to play with swimmers, who called him Beaky.

STRANDING

Sometimes either single whales or groups of whales swim on to shore, where they are **stranded**. Exactly why this happens is unknown. Sometimes it may be caused by disease or injury. If a sick whale becomes stranded, the other members of its group may try so hard to help it that they too become stranded. Often though, what appear to be perfectly healthy

This sperm whale is one of six that was stranded on a beach in north-east Scotland. Sadly, all six of these whales died.

whales become stranded. It can be difficult to save stranded whales. Their weight makes all but the smallest ones difficult to move. Their skin dries and cracks when it is out of water. Sadly, stranded whales that are rescued often strand themselves again soon after.

Threats and conservation

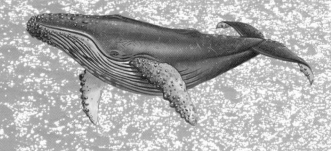

In the Antarctic summer of 1930–31, 30,000 blue whales were killed by whale hunters.

In the traditional whale hunt held in the Faeroe Islands, a school of pilot whales is driven ashore and killed.

Until vegetable substitutes became available, whale oil was used to make margarine.

Nets set by Japanese fishermen to catch salmon may cause the death by drowning of over 10,000 Dall's porpoises every year.

Without doubt, the greatest threat to whales has been from the **whaling** industry. Whales are a good source of meat and oil. People around the world have hunted whales for centuries, but they did not threaten the survival of any whale **species** until the second half of the 19th century. During that time, ways of killing whales became more efficient, and this led to the setting up of **whaling stations** and **factory ships** in the Antarctic and other parts of the world during the first half of the 20th century.

This fin whale is being cut up and processed in a whaling station in south-west Iceland.

Environmental pollution

Coastal dolphins and porpoises are threatened by
pollution that either comes from the land, or is caused
by ships leaking pollutants (substances that pollute) at
sea. The beluga whales that live in the Gulf of St Lawrence
in Canada have high levels of poisons in their bodies.
Many of these have come from **prey** such as eels that have
travelled from lakes polluted with industrial waste to the **estuary**,
where they are eaten by the whales.

I DIDN'T KNOW THAT

At its height, the whaling industry
killed tens of thousands of the
large **baleen whales** every year.
Blue, grey and right whales were
caught in such large numbers that
these species were in danger of
dying out. Now they are
protected, but there are still not as
many whales alive today as there
were before the whaling industry
was set up.

Some smaller whales are now in
danger of becoming **extinct** due to
habitat changes, pollution and
overfishing. The Indus river
dolphin and the Gulf porpoise are
under threat because changes
people have made to the flow of
the Indus and Colorado rivers have
destroyed their natural habitats.
Today, many organizations work to
protect all species of whales.

41

TRADITIONAL WHALE HUNTERS

In places such as the Faeroe Islands, Siberia, Alaska and the Caribbean islands of St Vincent and the Grenadines, whale hunting has taken place for hundreds of years. Today, most of the people who live in these places do not need whale products to survive, or even to earn a living. However, many of them consider **whaling** to be an important part of their way of life. In other parts of the world, many people feel that killing any whale is cruel and unnecessary.

OTHER THREATS

Dolphins and porpoises can become tangled up in fishing nets and lines that are not intended to harm them. Unable to reach the

This is the scene of a pilot whale hunt in the Faeroe Islands. The Faeroese consider the hunt an important part of their culture. Others think it should be banned.

surface to breathe, the trapped animals drown before the nets are brought to the surface. 'Dolphin-friendly' fishing gear helps to stop this happening, but some dolphins and porpoises are still dying in nets put out to catch squid and tuna.

INTERNATIONAL WHALING COMMISSION

The International Whaling Commission was created in 1946 to make sure the whaling industry obeyed rules. At first, the Commission was more concerned with making sure the industry had a good future. By the 1970s, the conservation (protection) of whales had become an important issue. In 1982 the Commission agreed to stop all whaling for a time. This finally began working in 1986, although a few countries, such as Japan, were allowed to catch small numbers of whales such as minkes for scientific reasons.

WHALE CONSERVATION

The Whale and Dolphin Conservation Society, Save the Whales and Greenpeace are just three of the many organizations that work to see that no **species** of whale becomes **extinct**. This work is called conservation. These organizations make people aware of threats to whales. In the case of Greenpeace, they sometimes take direct action at sea to stop whale hunting. We owe it to the people of the future to do all that we can now to stop any species of whale from becoming extinct.

Television programmes and conservation organizations have done a lot to teach people about threats to the future survival of whales.

Glossary

ancestor animal or person that lived long ago, from whom present-day animals are descended

baleen whale whale that has tough plates, called baleen, hanging from each side of the upper jaw instead of teeth. The plates are used to strain food from sea water.

beaked whale name of a group of species of medium-sized whales with long snouts

blowhole nostril or nostrils on a whale's head through which the animal breathes

blubber thick layer of fat under a whale's skin that covers most of its body

breaching when a whale throws itself clear of the water, then lands with a huge splash

calf young whale

captivity confined to a certain area. Animals in zoos or aquariums are in captivity.

carnivore animal that eats flesh

dorsal fin single fin found on the back of most whales

echolocation way in which a whale uses sound to navigate and find food in dark water

equator imaginary line around the middle of Earth, equally distant from the North and South Poles

estuary mouth of a large river

extinct when no more animals of a species remain alive

factory ship ship used as a base for a whaling fleet and where dead whales are taken

flukes pair of fins on the whale's tail that it uses to push itself through the water

habitat type of place, or environment that suits specific plants or animals

ice floe sheet of floating ice

identify recognize

mammal animal that is warm-blooded and feeds its young on milk

mate (verb) joining together of a male and female to produce young (offspring)

mate (noun) one of a male and female pair that have joined together to produce young

migration seasonal movement of animals from one area to another

mucus slimy substance made and given off by animals

nitrogen colourless, tasteless gas in the air we breathe

oxygen colourless, tasteless gas in the air we breathe. All animals need oxygen to stay alive.

plankton small fish and other tiny animals that drift in oceans, lakes, and rivers

polar describes something near the North or South Poles

pollute damage the environment with substances that are harmful to life

predator animal that hunts another animal for food

prey animal that is caught and eaten by another animal

rorqual name given to six whale species that have expanding grooves under the throat

school large group of fish, whales or dolphins travelling together

species kind or type of animal

spy-hopping when whales stand upright in the water in order to look around

stranding when whales swim on to or near shore and cannot get back to deep water

streamlined having a smooth shape that helps to move through air or water easily

toothed whales whales that have teeth rather than plates of baleen

tropical describes the hot regions near the equator where plants grow all year round

unique different from any other

warm-blooded animals that are able to maintain a constant body temperature

whaling hunting and killing whales

whaling station place on land where whale bodies are cut up and processed

Further information

Books

Animal Groups: Life in a Pod: Whales, Louise & Richard Spilsbury (Heinemann Library, 2003)

Eyewitness Books: Whale, Vassili Papastavrou (Dorling Kindersley, 2000)

Sea Creatures: Dolphins, Elizabeth Laskey (Heinemann Library, 2003)

Sea Creatures: Whales, Elizabeth Laskey (Heinemann Library, 2003)

Usborne Discovery: Whales and Dolphins (Internet-linked), Susannah Davidson (Usborne Publishing Ltd, 2002)

Websites

www.wdcs.org: the website for the Whale and Dolphin Conservation Society

www.enchantedlearning.com : search for 'whales'

www.bbc.co.uk/nature/wildfacts : search for 'whales'

www.yahooligans.com : search for 'whales'

Disclaimer

All the Internet addresses (URLs) given in this book were valid at the time of going to press. However, due to the dynamic nature of the Internet, some addresses may have changed, or sites may have ceased to exist since publication. While the author and publishers regret any inconvenience this may cause readers, no responsibility for any such changes can be accepted by either the author or the publishers.

Index

Numbers in *italic* indicate pictures

Titles in the Secret World of series include:

Hardback   1 844 21583 0

Hardback   1 844 21584 9

Hardback   1 844 21588 1

Hardback   1 844 21585 7

Hardback   1 844 21589 X

Hardback   1 844 21590 3

Hardback   1 844 21586 5

Hardback   1 844 21591 1

Find out about the other titles in this series on our website www.raintreepublishers.co.uk